T-BALL

Written by
Claudette C. Mitchell, Gracie R. Porter and Patricia Tefft Cousin
Illustrated by
James R. Threalkill and Michael J. McBride

I pick up the bat.

I step up to the plate.

I hit the ball. Homerun!

I run to first base.

I run to second base.

I run to third base.

And then I'm home!